Buying Multi Family Homes for Investment with Homes for sale in California

How to Run a Rental Property Business

Shawn Mahoney

TABLE OF CONTENTS

www.ingramcontent.com/pod-product-compliance
Lightning Source LLC
Chambersburg PA
CBHW011158220326
41597CB00028BA/4706

DEDICATION

**This book is dedicated to Stephanie Tam
A blessing from God and a good friend.**

ACKNOWLEDGMENTS

I WOULD LIKE TO ACKNOWLEDGE ALL THE HARD WORK OF THE MEN AND WOMEN OF THE UNITED STATES MILITARY, WHO RISK THEIR LIVES ON A DAILY BASIS, TO MAKE THE WORLD A SAFER PLACE.

Disclaimer

This book was written as a guide to starting a business. As with any other high yielding action, starting a business has a certain degree of risk. This book is not meant to take the place of accounting, legal, financial or other professional advice. If advice is needed in any of these fields, you are advised to seek the services of a professional.

While the author has attempted to make the information in this book as accurate as possible, no guarantee is given as to the accuracy or currency of any individual item. Laws and procedures related to business are constantly changing.

Therefore, in no event shall Brian Mahoney or MahoneyProducts Publishers be liable for any special, indirect, or consequential damages or any damages whatsoever in connection with the use of the information herein provided.

Chapter 1

Rental Property Investing Overview

Rental Property Investing Overview

Rental Property Investing is purchasing investment property for the purpose of renting it out for positive cash flow. It can be single family homes, mulitifamily units, apartment complexes or commercial property.

One of the biggest advantages of rental property investing, is getting passive income. Having your property or investment work for you, and earn a income while you relax or move on to other projects. If done properly, rental property investing can give you the freedom to live life on your terms and set your own schedule.

Rental Property Investing advantages:

* You don't have to be present to make money. You can purchase a home and have the rest of the work subcontracted out, and earn positive cash flow.

* Rental property investing allows you to make money in a variety of ways. You can earn appreciation on your property value and have your equity grow. You get tax benefits, interest and business write offs for property ownership. You can get positive cash flow income from your tenant's rent.

* You have a variety of business models to choose from. Single Family, Mulitfamily or Commercial property.

Rental Property Investing Overview

* Real Estate Investing is one of the most sound and enduring businesses ever created. When I was a child, JC Penny's and Sears were the retail giants. They have been replaced by Amazon and Walmart. Real Estate investing however, will always be around because people will always need a place to stay.

* The principles for success are easy to understand. Buy at or below wholesale, rehab if necessary, rent or flip for a profit.

When you start a rental property business, begin with the end in mind. What strategy do you want to use? There are several types of strategies to decide on. For example:

* What type of property do you want to invest in? Single family, multifamily, commercial lease, apartments, condos or duplexes?

* How much money do you want to earn? Knowing that number will help you to decide what type of property you want to invest in.

* How will you finance your properties? High interest loans from private lenders? Deal with the regulations of traditional lenders or how about using credit cards?

Rental Property Investing Overview

* Where do you want to invest? Many suggest you start out, witnin one hour of where you live. But if you have really big financial goals, you may decide to invest nationwide.

* What is your time frame? "Dreams are goals with a deadline." Tony Robbins. You have to make a list of goals that are accompanied with deadlines.

* Are you going to manage your properties or hire a property management company?

* All business ventures involve risk. Expect the best, prepare for the worst. Business liability insurance will help, as well as the decisions you make involving financing and tenant selection.

* Vacancy. Eventually a tenant will move out. What model of marketing will you use to buffer the lost of a tenant.

* Passive income is not passive, if you are working on everything. How much are you going to delegate or subcontract out?

Once you select your overall rental property investment strategies you have to put a team together. You will need an attorney, accountant, real estate agent, repair man or maintenance person and a marketing person.

Rental Property Investing Overview

When you select an attorney make sure he or she specializes in real estate. They have to have a detailed knowledge of real estate contracts that are fair and protect you.

When it comes to accounting there are tons of software options out there that might persuade you to do your own accounting. You have to decide how much responsibility you want to have when it comes to accounting.

If you have a good real estate agent, they are well worth their commission. The best real estate agents work full time. They are more motivated because their dinner depends on their success. They should be able to give you accurate comps (comps is short for Comparables. It is a real estate appraisal term referring to properties that are similar, that have sold recently in the same area) and have a deep understanding of the real estate market.

Whether it's a single family, or much larger property, you should have a maintenance or repair person. Depending on the size of your business, you may need to have several maintenance personnel. If you decide to hire subcontractors, use references to make sure they are reliable.

Rental Property Investing Overview

Marketing. With the growth of the internet, there are now tons of ways to market your property. Your marketing can be as simple as business cards and a web site. Or your marketing could also be as detailed as creating YouTube videos for marketing in combination with other forms of social media like Facebook Ads, email marketing, customer list building, article marketing and press releases.

"Study to show yourself approved, a workman that need not be ashamed." Make educated decisions based on sound knowledge (people are destroyed for lack of knowledge). Learn from your mistakes.

Practice patiences for your success. In the parable of the Chinises bamboo tree, speaker Les Brown teaches that the Chinese baboo tree has to be watered every day while it grows for 5 years underground. Then it reaches enormous heights, shortly after it bursts threw the ground. Continue to water your real estate dreams for your breaktrhrough.

Make a decision to be determined to succeed. Set your goals. Make a plan. Then take action. Nothing worthwile comes without challenges. Learn to enjoy the challenges, knowing that it is helping you to grow. After all, what's life without a little adventure?

Chapter 2

How To Purchase Investment Property

Expert Strategies to Purchase Property

Expert Strategies to Purchase Property

AVOIDING & MANAGING & ELIMINATING RISK

Legendary Real Estate investor Dave Del Dotto once said "stick with the government, they will make you rich.". Real Estate is one of the safest investments in the world, when done properly. There is risk just driving to the grocery store. The only thing separating you from a head on collision is a yellow strip of paint. That being said, there are risks in every financial investment decision you make.

Do your research. Know what you want to do, before you begin. Are you looking to flip properties? Hold on and make money on the interest rates? Are you looking for a property to live in? Are you looking to rent out properties? Each decision requires a different type of research. If you are looking to rent out properties then you need to research what the local apartment complexes and homes are renting for in the area. If you are looking to flip a property then you need to find a real estate agent that can give you comps that have sole in the area within the past year.

Visit any property you are going to purchase. You do not want to get stuck with swampland or a unbuildable lot.

Expert Strategies to Purchase Property

AVOIDING & MANAGING & ELIMINATING RISK

You also don't want to get stuck with a property that has high property taxes. Learn the property tax rates of all the counties in the state that you are going to invest in.

Make sure that the property has not been condemned.

Make sure that the property does not have numerous costly violations of city codes.

Ask multiple real estate agents for information on any area you are interested in investing.

Ask about possible environmental issues.

Research possible liens by builders and contractors.

Beware of a owner who may declare bankruptcy on a property. This is a manageable risk but because laws change constantly, consult a real estate attorney for more information on how to handle this risk.

Avoid scams by dealing with government employees as much as possible.

Expert Strategies to Purchase Property

1. Decide how much you can afford to invest and stick with the numbers you come up with. Avoid something called Auction fever. It can be started by a "fast hammer". A fast hammer is when the auctioneer closes the auction early at a amazing price. It is designed to get your attention and get a fever about being the next one in the room to get a "Great Deal". When you go to a auction you should have a list of properties you have research and what your bid is going to be. This will help you to avoid Auction Fever.

2. Research. Single family homes with at least 3 bedrooms are great investments if purchased at the right price. Your research tells you what the right price is. Remember to use real estate agents and their access to the multiple listing service. Also many big companies like Remax and Century 21 have websites up with tons of information on the real estate area you wish to invest in.

www.trulia.com

 www.zillow.com

www.biggerpockets.com

https://www.census.gov/quickfacts/table/PST045216/00

http://www.realtor.org

Those are just a few of the great sites to get research information on real estate.

Expert Strategies to Purchase Property

3. Get in contact with local counties for a list of delinquent properties for sale. Also ask when the sales will take place. Ask if you can be put on a mailing list. Use the internet to track down as much information as you can. Don't be afraid to use search engines other than Google. Bing and Yahoo are also great search engines to use.

4. Buy from other investors. Some people get in over their head. As long as you know the numbers and have research the property, it does not matter who you purchase it from as long as it is a good deal. One investor in Michigan recently purchased every single property for sale at a tax auction. He has to sell those properties or he is responsible for paying the taxes. As Carelton Sheets once said "you can't rationalize murder" so how can you rationalize why someone might offer you a great deal? Just do your due diligence on the property before making a deal.

5. Establish a relationship with local officials. Learn the names of the people who work in government offices that will be giving you information. Visit in person and say thank you. Call and say thank you. Send them a card that says thank you. How many people do you think do that for them? They will remember you. I worked for the government for over 20 years. I still remember the woman who repeatedly gave me lemon-aid when it was hot outside.

6. Buy early in the Year. When you buy a tax lien certificate, back taxes have to be paid to the treasurer as well as interest and penalties. Redeem the property and you could be earning interest on this larger amount of money. If the property is not redeemed you can turn in the tax lien certificate and be handed a deed for the property, any extra amount you pay for the certificate comes from you because you could have gotten the same property for less.

7. Try smaller counties you may have much less competition.

8. Invest in your comfort zone. Try to find mentors who have already done what it is you want to do. As your knowledge and experience increases then you can take on bigger projects.

9. Write down your goals. Remember to answer the question of why you are doing this in the first place. A powerful why will keep you motivated when it comes time to do the legwork required to be successful.

10. Take Action. There are plenty of smart people who are poor. Proper Knowledge plus action is the key to success.

Expert Strategies to Purchase Property

In microeconomics total cost (TC) describes the total economic cost of production and is made up of variable costs, which vary according to the quantity of a good produced and include inputs such as labor and raw materials, plus fixed costs.

In English... you factor in as many external costs, not just the cost of the investment property.

In order to be successful when buying investment property, you have to be good at determining the Total Cost of a property.

11. Get Investment Property Market Value

Wholesale Real Estate is real estate that is real estate priced under it's retail value. But how do you know that the retail value of real estate property? The standard formula for finding the value of real estate is to have a real estate agent find comparable (comps) properties that have sold recently. Usually about 4 properties with in a mile of the purchase property, that have sold within the past year. Formulas vary from bank to bank and real estate agent to real estate agent.

Today you can get a rough estimate by doing the research yourself. Remember that a bank will probably use their own formula, but at least you can try to get a ball park figure of a properties value by using these web sites.

Appraisal Web Sites

https://www.zillow.com/how-much-is-my-home-worth/

http://www.eppraisal.com/

12. Selecting a Real Estate Agent

So now that you have found a property, researched it's value, it's time to make an offer. Some times you have to use a government approved agent to make an offer. Like any profession, there are good agents and not so good agents.

When I lived in Virginia, once a year the local paper published a list of all the top real estate agents for almost every real estate agent franchise/business. If your local paper does not do that then here is a formula I use for selecting a real estate agent.

Expert Strategies to Purchase Property

No part timers. Part time effort usually gets you part time results. I want an agent whose livelihood depends on their success.

Size Does Matter

The size that matters. The size or amount of properties sold. Not necessarily the gross amount of property value sold. Suppose you had a real estate agent who sold 1 million dollars worth of real estate and another who sold $500,000 worth of real estate. Which one do you choose? It depends. I want the agent who has sold the most individual properties, and not necessary the one who has the highest gross. An agent can sell only 1 house for a million dollars. The agent who sold $500,000 worth of real estate may have sold 10 $50,000 homes.

Usually a agent who makes a lot of sales has a good marketing formula in place and a good team of agents working with or for her/him. Don't be afraid to ask "who's your best agent? Why?". Often a real estate company will try to toss their worst agent a bone. Don't be that bone. Remember they work for you. Their commission comes from the property you are investing in.

Some courses teach you to negotiate the commission. I believe a proficient agent is worth the commission they desire. It's your job to select a proficient agent.

Expert Strategies to Purchase Property

13. "100-3" Formula

Here is a quick and easy formula for getting a great deal on a real estate investment property, using a real estate agent that you have build up some rapport with.

Have the agent find 100 properties for sale that have been on the market for at least 90 days. Have the agent fax an offer of 25% below market value to all of the properties. Because the properties have been on the market for at least 90 days, you are dealing with motivated sellers. It is likely that 10 out of the 100 will accept your offer. Now filter through the 10 and select the best 3 properties. Use these filters to help you select the best 3.

Strategies To Making Offers

1. What are the property taxes?

2. Are there any Homeowner Association dues?

3. What will be the appreciation value?

4. What will be your utility expenses.

5. How much will it cost, to be "live-in" ready.

6. Is it the lowest valued house in the neighboorhood?

7. What is the Crime Rate

Expert Strategies to Purchase Property

Property Taxes

I once owned two homes free and clear. The homes were in the same state. Both were similar in size, but one had a $3,000 a year property tax and the other one was $300 a year in property taxes. You can guess which one I moved first. Property taxes are often overlooked, but can be a big factor in the (TC) total cost. Do your research before you make an offer.

HOA (Home Owner Association)

Usually when a house seems like the perfect deal, but has been sitting on the market for a long time, look to see what the HOA dues are. Personally I stay away from any property that has HOA dues, because they can escalate and you have no control over them.

Appreciation

Look at the history of real estate appreciation. It can vary greatly form city to city, and neighborhood to neighborhood. If you are going for a quick flip then this is not that important.

Utility Expenses

The importance of the expense depends on what you are going to do with the property.

Expert Strategies to Purchase Property

Rehab Expenses

If you are not an expert, have a professional inspect the house so you can factor in, a accurate estimate of rehab expenses. Be aware of any possible code violations as well.

Cost relative to the Neighborhood

Usually it's easiest to sell the cheapest house in the most expensive neighborhood. However if you just plan on renting the house then this is not as big a factor.

Crime Rate

The crime rate can have a big impact on resale value. Use web sites like https://www.crimereports.com/ to help understand it's impact on your property.

14. "Take what the defense gives you"

Take what the defense gives you is a sports metaphor for viewing the landscape of a situation and adapting to what you see.

Take a similar approach to making offers in real estate. If you tell a "For Sale By Owner" everything that is wrong with the house he or she spend a lifetime building... you may insult the owner and lose the deal.

However, you send a list of needed repairs to a HUD representative, he may reduce the price of the property, no questions asked.

Adjust your offer making strategy to the person or organization you are dealing with. The farther removed a person is from the property, the less emotional they are about making deals.

Know your profit numbers and stick to them. Especially if you are bidding on a property. Be aware of Auction fever. It will bring out the competitive nature in you and can lead to you over bidding on a property. Know your numbers and be disciplined. The reason you pick out 3 properties in the 100-3 formula is so that you have 2 other properties to go to, if your first choice does not work out.

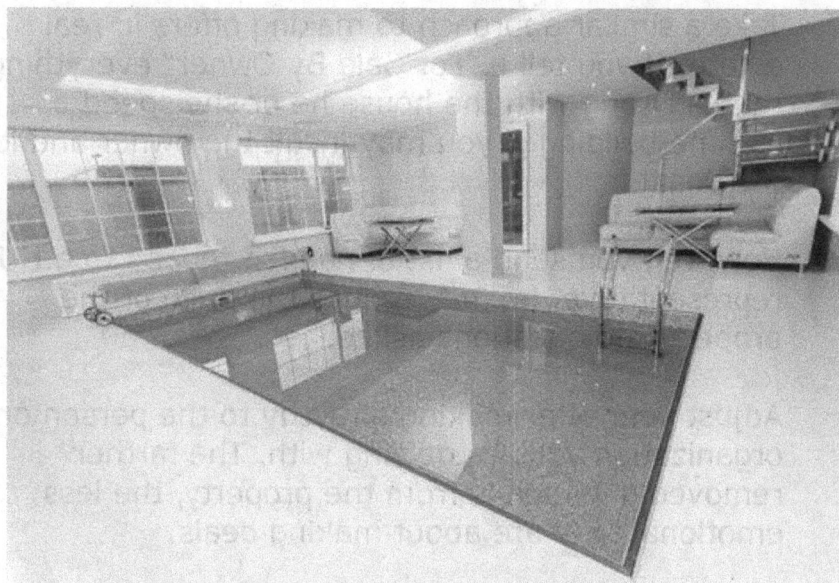

Chapter 3

Finding Discount Property in California Counties

California Cash Flow Counties of Wholesale Property!

The internet has made it possible to grow your real estate investing business quickly and easily. Now you can view hundreds of properties online without ever leaving your home.

In this chapter I am going to give you a ton of web sites and the addresses to government wholesale sources, to help you to cover this state's real estate goldmines. I have selected some of the biggest counties with the largest supply of wholesale real estate.

In general you should look at 100 homes for every 1 property that you purchase. Comparing factors like the home value, rent potential, repair cost, local taxes, possible home owner fees, utilities etc...

While there is no substitute for inspecting a home in person, having access to thousands of homes on the internet can help you to narrow down the field to spectacular deals! So take advantage of this knowledge to help secure your real estate investing success!

California Cash Flow Counties of Wholesale Property!

Locate Statewide California Properties

MLS.com

http://www.mls.com/search/California.mvc

California Real Estate Foreclosures with links to different cities on the landing page.

REALTOR.com

http://www.realtor.com/foreclosures/California

Links to California real estate properties by county and city.

Top California Counties

The previous web sites give you access to a broad selection of property in all the counties in California.

Next I narrow it down to a handful of the top counties based on the population size, rising property values, rental profit potential and the abundance of wholesale property available.

California Cash Flow Counties of Wholesale Property!

1. Los Angeles County

Los Angeles County has a population of 10,170,292 and is 4,060 square miles. In this county there are a large amount of Goldmine real estate investment oppurtunities.

Tax Property Info Street Address:

Los Angeles County Treasurer and Tax Collector

500 W. Temple St., Room 225, Los Angeles, CA 90012 Phone: (213) 974-2111 or (888) 807-2111

Foreclosures web Address:

https://www.realtor.com/foreclosures/Los-Angeles-County_CA

Tax Sales web site:

https://ttc.lacounty.gov/schedule-of-upcoming-auctions/

Auction and Sale of Tax-Defaulted Property

213.974.2045

auction@ttc.lacounty.gov

2. San Diego County

San Diego County has a population of 3,299,521 and is 4,204 square miles.

Tax Property Info Street Address:

San Diego County Treasurer and Tax Collector

1600 Pacific Hwy, Room 162, San Diego, CA 92101-2474   Phone: (877) 829-4732

Government property information :

Probate Property:

(858) 694-3500 or email
Noel.Agarma@sdcounty.ca.gov

Surplus Property:

https://urlzs.com/R1CLc

Sheriff sales:

https://www.sdsheriff.net/courts/property-sales.html

Tax Sales web site:

https://urlzs.com/q4Qny

California Cash Flow Counties of Wholesale Property!

3. Orange County

Orange County has a population of 3,169,776 and is 790 square miles.

Tax Property Info Street Address:

Orange County Treasurer and Tax Collector

12 Civic Center Plaza, Bldg 12, Santa Ana 92701

Phone: (714) 834-3411

Foreclosures web Address:

https://urlzs.com/ubXKc

Tax Sales web site:

http://www.ttc.ocgov.com/proptax/pta/

California Cash Flow Counties of Wholesale Property!

4. Riverside County

Riverside County has a population of 2,361,026 and is 7,208 square miles.

Tax Property Info Street Address:

Riverside County Treasurer and Tax Collector

P.O. Box 12005, Riverside, CA 92502-2205

Phone: (951) 955-3900 Fax: (951) 955-3906

Foreclosures web Address:

https://urlzs.com/ogMzP

Tax Sales web site:

https://www.countytreasurer.org/TaxCollector/TaxSaleInformati
on.aspx

California Cash Flow Counties of Wholesale Property!

5. San Bernardino County

San Bernardino County has a population 2,128,133 and is 20,000   square miles.

Tax Property Info Street Address:

San Bernardino County Tax Collector

172 West Third Street, First Floor, San Bernardino, CA 92415-0360

Phone: (909) 387-8308

Foreclosures web Address:

https://urlzs.com/AzNAJ

Tax Sales web site:

https://urlzs.com/4ueXS

California Cash Flow Counties of Wholesale Property!

6. Santa Clara County

Santa Clara County has a population of 1,918,044 and is 1,291 square miles.

Tax Property Info Street Address:

Santa Clara County Tax Collector's Office

70 West Hedding Street, East Wing, 6th Floor, San Jose, CA 95110

Phone: (408) 808-7900

Sheriff's Sale:

https://urlzs.com/TqNRi

Tax Sales web site:

https://urlzs.com/JsMB8

Find California Wholesale
Real Estate Fast!

7. Sacramento County

Sacramento County has a population of 1,501,335 and is 966 square miles.

Tax Property Info Street Address:

Sacramento County Department of Finance, Tax Collection Division

700 H Street, Room 1710, Sacramento, CA 95814

Phone: (916) 874-6622

Government Real Property:

https://urlzs.com/Y6Bzj

Tax Sales web site:

https://urlzs.com/2aB8X

Chapter 4

Finding Discount Property in California Cities

California Real Estate Investing

City Goldmines

1. Los Angeles

The city of Los Angeles has a population of 3,949,776 to support your real estate investing business.

The **median home value** in Los Angeles is $686,100. Los Angeles is a real estate goldmine city because recently the home values have gone up 2.2 percent and is expected to lower only -.1 percent.

Houses currently listed in Los Angeles have a median list price of about $829,994. Homes that actually sold have a median price of about $706,900.

The **median rent price** in Los Angeles is about $3,500 a month.

Foreclosure Warning sign

Delinquent mortgages in Los Angeles is .7 percent. The *Foreclosure potiential rank is #3 between California goldmine cities.*

California Real Estate Investing

City Goldmines

2. San Diego

The city of San Diego has a population of 1,390,966 to support your real estate investing business.

The **median home value** in San Diego is $633,600. San Diego is a real estate goldmine city because recently the home values have gone up 1.7 percent and is expected to rise at least another 0.2 percent.

Houses currently listed in San Diego have a median list price of about $705,000. Homes that actually sold have a median price of about $601,300.

The **median rent price** in San Diego is about $2,750 a month.

Foreclosure Warning sign

Delinquent mortgages in San Diego is .4 percent. The *Foreclosure potiential rank is #6 between California goldmine cities.*

California Real Estate Investing

City Goldmines

3. San Francisco

The city of San Francisco has a population of 864,263 to support your real estate investing business.

The median home value in San Francisco is $1,357,500. San Francisco is a real estate goldmine city because recently the home values have gone up 3.0 percent and is expected to fall only -.1 percent.

Houses currently listed in San Francisco have a median price of about $1,299,000.

The median rent price in San Francisco is about $4,506 a month.

Foreclosure Warning sign

Delinquent mortgages in San Francisco is .2 percent. The *Foreclosure potiential rank is #7 the least among the California goldmine cities.*

California Real Estate Investing
City Goldmines

4. Fresno

The city of Fresno has a population of 519,037 to support your real estate investing business.

The median home value in Fresno is $242,500. Fresno is a real estate goldmine city because recently the home values have gone up 6.5 percent and is expected to rise at least another 3.6 percent.

Houses currently listed in Fresno have a median price of about $284,900. Homes that actually sold have a median list price of about $249,800.

The median rent price in Fresno is about $1,400 a month.

Foreclosure Warning sign

Delinquent mortgages in Fresno is 1.1 percent. The *Foreclosure potiential rank is #2 between California goldmine cities.*

5. Sacramento

The city of Sacramento has a population of 489,650 to support your real estate investing business.

The median home value in Sacramento is $326,900. Sacramento is a real estate goldmine city because recently the home values have gone up 4.3 percent and is expected to rise at least another 1.9 percent.

Houses currently listed in Sacramento have a median price of about $330,000. Homes that actually sold have a median list price of about $315,100.

The median rent price in Sacramento is about $1,750 a month.

Foreclosure Warning sign

Delinquent mortgages in Sacramento is .7 percent. The *Foreclosure potiential rank is #3 between California goldmine cities.*

California Real Estate Investing

City Goldmines

6. Long Beach

The city of Long Beach has a population of 470,489 to support your real estate investing business.

The median home value in Long Beach is $593,500. Long Beach is a real estate goldmine city because recently the home values have gone up 2.0 percent and is expected to rise at least another .3 percent.

Houses currently listed in Long Beach have a median price of about $599,000. Homes that actually sold have a median list price of about $557,300.

The median rent price in Long Beach is about $2,300 a month.

Foreclosure Warning sign

Delinquent mortgages in Long Beach is .6 percent. The *Foreclosure potiential rank is #5 between California goldmine cities.*

7. Bakersfield

The city of Bakersfield has a population of 372,680 to support your real estate investing business.

The median home value in Bakersfield is $241,600. Bakersfield is a real estate goldmine city because recently the home values have gone up 5.2 percent and is expected to rise at least another 2.6 percent.

Houses currently listed in Bakersfield have a median price of about $276,700. Homes that actually sold have a median list price of about $249,300.

The median rent price in Bakersfield is about $1,500 a month.

Foreclosure Warning sign

Delinquent mortgages in Bakersfield is 1.5 percent. Bakersfield has the greatest foreclosure *potiential of the California goldmine cities and is ranked #1 in that category.*

7. Bakersfield

The city of Bakersfield has a population of 372,550 to support your real estate investing business.

The median home value in Bakersfield is $241,600. Bakersfield is a real estate goldmine city because recently the home values have gone up 3.2 percent and is expected to rise at least another 2.5 percent.

CHAPTER 5

Creative Real Estate Financing Techniques

4,000 sources For money!

FINANCING REAL ESTATE

Welcome to Expert financing. I am going to show you several realistic ways to finance real estate. You are going to learn how to finance real estate with.

* VA LOANS

* PARTNERS

* INVESTMENT CLUBS

* CREDIT CARDS

* CORPORATE CREDIT

* EQUITY

* SELLER FINANCE

* HARD MONEY LENDERS

* AND FINALLY I SHOW YOU THE MONEY$!!

USING A VA LOAN

According to the web sites www.benefits.va.gov and www.military.com the current VA Loan amount is a whopping $417,000! What a lot of veterans don't know is that you can use that money to purchase not only your home, but investment properties. That is how I started my investing career. Purchasing multiple homes using my VA Loan.

FINANCING REAL ESTATE

Even if you are not a veteran, you can still partner up with one, who still has some money left on his or her VA LOAN.

If you are a Veteran, you will need to obtain a copy of your DD 214 and VA Form 26-1880 Request for a Certificate of Eligibility.

PARTNERS

This is another way I purchased a home. At the time I worked for the United States Postal Service. I had already purchased plenty of homes, so many of the workers were aware I had successfully invested in real estate. At break time I went around and ask people to partner up with me. I had multiple people offer to go in as a partner. I choose one and that house we rehabbed and flipped just two months after purchasing it. To this day it was the biggest gross profit on one deal, I have had. True I had to split it with my partner, but I would rather have half of something than all of nothing.

Having the combined resources of two people can be a great benefit, but it is not without it's challenges. If you are going to use a partner, no matter how close you are...GET EVERY THING IN WRITING.

FINANCING REAL ESTATE

Having a partner can dramatically increase the chance of a Bank lending money as well as having someone to split the work on rehabbing, should you decide to save money and make repairs yourself. But all this must be spelled out BEFORE you enter into a Agreement/Contract and purchase a home.

It helps if the person is like minded and understands the risks and benefits of investing, and truly understands the return on investment of a particular deal.

REAL ESTATE INVESTMENT CLUBS

Real estate investment clubs are groups that meet locally and allow investors and other professionals to network and learn. They can provide extremely useful information for both the novice and expert real estate investor. A top real estate club can provide a great forum to network, learn about reputable contractors, brokers, realtors, lawyers, accountants and other professionals. On the other hand, there are many real estate clubs designed to sell you. They bring in "gurus" who sell either on stage or at the back of the room, and as a result, the clubs typically profit to the tune of %50 of the sale price of the product, bootcamp, or training that is pitched.

FINANCING REAL ESTATE

I have purchased a ton of real estate books and real estate courses. Carlton Sheets, Dave Del Dotto, The Mylands, Seminar courses and much much more. I am not against any club bringing in a speaker who has a course. However I think there should be transparency to the members of the club.

There is certainly value in the networking that may come at one of these groups. But attend working to attain your goals and not necessarily the club's goal to sell you something. Some times both are the same thing. As a rule I usually leave debit cards at home the first time I attend an event. If there is a seller there with a "This day only offer" then I won't feel pressured to purchase. Plus most sellers can be convinced to sell at the discount offer price at a later time when you have had a chance to come down off the "sense of urgency emotional pitch".

CREDIT CARDS

When using a credit card in real estate you must really do your homework on the deal. Dan Kennedy a world famous marketer once said "always stack the numbers in your favor". That's how you use a credit card. Look at the return on investment as compared to the long term cost of using a credit card and it's interest. Also I would recommend buying low cost homes that you can purchase and own free and clear.

FINANCING REAL ESTATE

No Mortgage Payment!!! My last 2 homes I have purchased have been cash deals. One home cost $1,500 and the other about $7,000. The first was a government property from HUD and the 2nd From a Bank. These institutions are unemotional about real estate and simply view a property as a non performing asset. The 2nd home was 4 bedrooms, 1 1/2 bath and a basement located in a farming community and came with a 2 car garage/shed and .6 acre(that is the size of a NFL football field) of land.

In this book I show you how to find plenty of houses with amazing below wholesale prices and a formula for almost always finding a great deal.

CORPORATE CREDIT

Many people set up corporations to buy and sell real estate as an additional protection against liabilities. Other's create a corporation to mask personal involvement in property transfers and public records. Regardless of the use of a corporation, you can buy real estate with corporate credit as an alternative to using your own cash or IRA. By capitalizing on the credit rating of your corporation, you can buy real estate and build your corporate holdings portfolio.

FINANCING REAL ESTATE

Just remember that you can set up your corporation in a state that favors you the most for your real estate deals. Do your research. Most people like Delaware and Nevada, but you will have to decide if your home state or any other state is best for you and your business.

CURRENT EQUITY

Using the equity in your home for real estate investing is another way you can finance properties. You might use the money for a down payment or it may only be enough to cover the cost of some rehab repairs.

If you stick to the low cost home formula, you may have enough to purchase the entire house. A house is an investment that should appreciate in value as well as give a great ROI (Return On Investment). When you decide to flip the property or rent it out for positive cashflow.

If you have equity and it's not doing anything, then you may decide to make it a "performing asset" and use it as part of your real estate finance program.

FINANCING REAL ESTATE

SELLER FINANCING

Seller finance is where the seller of a free and clear property becomes your bank along with being the seller.

Advantages:

You get to purchase the property on terms that may be more beneficial for you. Seller gets monthly payments and the benefit of treating the sale as an installment sale thus allowing them to defer any capital gains taxes that may be due.

Disadvantages:

You may be locked into a mortgage with a pre-payment penalty or may not be able to resell the property immediately. This strategy is typically not meant for flipping but can definitely be used for that purpose if structured correctly.

Seller Finance is a known way to finance a property. That is why I have presented it in this book. But it is my least favorite because you now have a lingering relationship with your property. Your ability to make decisions regarding the property is limited and for that reason, I would not go this route. However, like all types of financing, you have to ask yourself, "is the deal worth it."

FINANCING REAL ESTATE

I also prefer to work alone, but when a great deal came along, I sought out a partner to make it happen. Risk is usually relative to potential profit.

HARD MONEY LENDERS

A hard money lender is usually a individual or company that lends money for an investment secured by the investment property.

Advantages:

Less red tape to get the money. You are dealing with people who understand the real estate investment business.

Disadvantage:

This is not a long term loan. The lender wants a return on investment, usually within a few months, a a year, or a few years. The interest rate on the loan is much higher than usual conventional banks.

Using hard money has a higher risk because the return on investment is due quicker. Therefore it is a good idea not to use a Hard Money Lender, until you have a great deal of experience and confidence in being able to produce a return on investment.

SHOWING YOU THE MONEY

A list of web sites for financing.

www.businessfinance.com (4,000 sources of money!)

www.advanceamericaproperty.com

http://www.cashadvanceloan.com/

www.brookviewfinancial.com

www.commercialfundingcorp.com

www.dhlc.com
(hard money for the Texas area)

www.equity-funding.com

www.bankofamerica.com

www.carolinahardmoney.com
(for real estate investors in North and South
Carolina)

www.fpfloans.com

FINANCING REAL ESTATE

As you can see there are plenty of strategies for financing a property. Do your research on your investment property and get the true market value. Purchase well below wholesale. This will help to minimize risk and elevate your potential profit margins. Buying below wholesale also creates a buffer for unexpected expenses.

So don't let the lack of money be a roadblock in your real estate investing dreams.

As you can see there are plenty of strategies for financing a property. Do your research on your investment property and get the true market value. Purchase well below wholesale. This will help to minimize risk and elevate your potential profit margins. Buying below wholesale also creates a

Crowd Funding Crowd Sourcing

Chapter 6

CrowdFunding for Real Estate Investors

Crowd Funding Crowd Sourcing

In 2015 over $34 billion dollars was raised by crowdfunding. Crowdfunding and Crowdsourcing roots began in 2005 and they help to finance or fund projects by raising money from a large number of people, usually by using the internet.

This type of fundraising or venture capital usually has 3 components. The individual or organization with a project that needs funding, groups of people who donate to the project, and a organization sets up a structure or rules to put the two together.

These websites do charge fees. The standard fee for success is about %5. If your goal is not met there is also a fee.

Below is a list of the top Crowdfunding websites according to myself and Entrepreneur Magazine Contributor Sally Outlaw.

Crowd Funding Crowd Sourcing

https://www.indiegogo.com/

Started as a platform for getting movies made, now helps to raise funds for any cause.

http://rockethub.com/

Started as a platform for the arts, now it helps to raise funds for business, science, social projects and education.

http://peerbackers.com/

Peerbackers focuses on raising funds for business, entrepreneurs and innovators.

https://www.kickstarter.com/

The most popular and well know n of all the crowdfunding websites. Kickstarter focuses on film, music, technology, gaming, design and the creative arts. Kickstarter only accepts projects from the United States, Canada and the United Kingdom.

Crowd Funding Crowd Sourcing

Group Growvc

http://group.growvc.com/

This website is for business and technology innovation.

https://microventures.com/

Get access to angel investors. This website is for business startups.

https://angel.co/

Another website for business startups.

https://circleup.com/

Circle up is for innovative consumer companies.

https://www.patreon.com/

If you start a YouTube Channel (highly recommended) you will hear about this website frequently. This website is for creative content people.

Crowd Funding Crowd Sourcing

https://www.crowdrise.com/

"Raise money for any cause that inspires you."
The Landing page slogan speaks for itself. #1
fundraising website for personal causes.

https://www.gofundme.com/

This fundraising website allows for business, charity,
education, emergencies, sports, medical, memorials,
animals, faith, family, newlyweds etc...

https://www.youcaring.com/

The leader in free fundraising. Over $400 million
raised.

https://fundrazr.com/

FundRazr is an award-winning online fundraising
platform that has helped thousands of people and
organizations raise money
for causes they care about.

Chapter 7

How to start Rehabbing Houses

Rehabbing Real Estate

There are three basic components to rehabbing a property. Have a property inspection, a cost analysis and hire a contractor.

A. Home Inspection

You can hire a licensed professional to inspect the propery or you can do it yourself. I advise hiring a licensed professional with a great deal of experience.

To hire a professional you can google "home inspection, your city, your state" or go to homeadvisor.com.

http://www.homeadvisor.com/

https://goo.gl/vL4gWK

If you choose to do it yourself here is a basic home inspection checklist.

Rehabbing Real Estate

Exterior

* Roof: Determine if the roof needs repairs or needs to be replaced.

* Lawn: Determine what kind of landscaping is needed or if the yard needs to be reseeded.

* Sprinkler: Is there a sprinkler system? If so does it work?

* Lights: Do the lights work? Are there motion sensors? Are there cost efficient bulbs?

* Outlets: Do the outlets work?

* Fence: Does it need repair or painting?

* Trees: Do any trees need to be removed or trimmed?

* Garage Door: Does it open and close easily?

Rehabbing Real Estate

Overall Interior

* **Walls:**   Do they need paint or repair?

* **Floors:**   Do tiles or carpet need to be replaced? Do wood floors need to be repaired?

* **Stairs:**   Are the stairs sturdy? Do they make noise. Is the handrail sturdy and safe?

* **Outlets:**   Purchase a voltage tester and see if all the outlets work.

* **Doors:**   Do they open and close easily? Are they level?

* **Windows:**   Do you feel any breezes when you stand by them? Are they cost efficient?

* **Lights:**   Turn on every light switch to make sure they work. (Note: If the home is unoccupied and the power is turned off, this won't be possible.)

Rehabbing Real Estate

Kitchen

* **Countertops:** Check for chips and cracks.

* **Cabinets:** Do they open and close easily? Do they need to be refinished or replaced?

* **Oven:** Does the oven work? Is it outdated?

* **Refrigerator:** Check to see if it freezes. Does it pass the eyeball test or is it an eyesore.

* **Faucet:** Run the water in the sink. Any leaks? How is the water pressure?

* **Range Hood:** See if the range hood fan and light work. It most likely will need to be cleaned.

Bathrooms

* **Plumbing/Drainage:** Fill up the sink and tub and see how the water drains out.

* **Faucets:** Check for leaks.

* **Toilet:** Is there enough pressure when it is flushed?

* **Bath Tub:** Is it too small? Any scratches?

* **Ventilation:** Does the fan work? Is there a window? Does it open and close easily?

Bedrooms

* **Closets:** Is there enough space? Are hanger rods needed?

Rehabbing Real Estate

Living/Dining/Family Room

* Ceiling Fans: Do ceiling fans need to be added or replaced?

Basement

* Mold: If there is an odor, check for mold and mildew.

* Furnace: Does the furnace work? Is it outdated? Up to code?

* Water Heater: Check for water around the base of the water heater. Any stickers on this to indicate installation date?

A documentary about Walt Disney revealed that Walt purchased a home for his parents and a faulty gas furnace was the cause of his mother's death. So inspecting a house can be a life or death matter.

You can use this checklist to determine your offer price and begin a overall cost analysis. However it is highly recommended that you use a professional.

B. Cost Analysis

When investing in real estate, you should always stack the numbers in your favor. If you can purchase a property at %50 of it's wholesale value, then you leave enough margin for error to absorb expenses and still sell the property for a profit.

The real estate web site biggerpockets.com has a investment calculator that can do the cost analysis work for you.

https://www.biggerpockets.com/real-estate-investment-calculator

https://goo.gl/HFoK9x

Rehabbing Real Estate

However you can do a quick cost analysis yourself.
Here are the basic numbers you will need.

* after repair value

* desired profit

* estimated repair cost

* purchase closing cost

* sale closing cost

* agent commission

* monthly holding costs

* number of days it will take to rehab and sell

Take the "after repair value" and substract all of the
expenses.

C. Hire a Contractor

It is a good idea that you hire a contractor. However if you decide to do the repair work yourself there is a supply discount program from Home Depot.

WHAT IS IT?

You have to get their Pro Xtra Account. If you're spending at least $1,500, chances are you can save money. In select markets, you may only need to spend only $1,000. Check with your local store to confirm required purchase amount.

HOW DOES IT WORK?

Assemble your project list. Build your cart in the store. If your total adds up to at least $1,500 (or $1,000 in select markets, check with your local store), you probably qualify for a volume discount.

Quotes can be processed by the Pro Desk any time and most requests are priced immediately. Membership in Pro Xtra Loyalty Program is required to receive discounts.

Full details are at the web site listed below...

http://www.homedepot.com/c/Pro_VolumePricing

Rehabbing Real Estate

A. How to Find a good Contractor

Go to your local building material warehouses like Lowes, Home Depot, Menards and Sherwin Williams.

Ask them who are their high volume contractors. If contracters are frequently purchasing supplies then they are frequently working. This is one of the more reliable ways to find a quality contractor.

Ask other contractors. Often times you will come across a good contractor who is busy on another project. Ask him/her for recommendations.

Ask a high volume real estate agent. Top real estate agents usually know one or two good contractors.

Use the internet.

Google "contractors, your city, your state".

Use homeadvisor.com

Try angieslist.com

Rehabbing Real Estate

B. Contractor Checklist

Hiring the right contractor can make or break a deal. Remember they work for you, so don't be shy about asking questions and getting proof, BEFORE you sign a contract. Here is a question checklist.

1. Do you have a license bond and insurance?

Do You Carry General Liability Insurance?

- It is Best to find a remodel contractor that carries general liability insurance.

2. Do you have referrals?

Do not hesitate to call referrals. - Nice to get several customer references from the last 6 months to one year.

3. Can I get a detailed and comprehensive scope of work with the bid?

4. Ask about experience and verify if you can.

5. Who's doing the work and who's going to be the daily contact on the project?

- Make sure the contractor or his foreman is on the job whenever work is being performed.

6. Will You Pull All the Required Building Permits?

- Pulling the required building permits, you know things will be done to "code."

7. Do You Guarantee Your Work?

Your contractor should guarantee his work for at least one year from date of completion. They should also include any warranties from the material used if applicable.

8. How do you handle clean up?

Clean up can be expensive. You need to know if the best options are being used.

9. How Is Payment Handled?

- Per job?

- Upon completion?

- Weekly?

- Some money upfront?

- Do you have capital to buy materials in case we need you to?

These are basic questions that you should be asking to interview contractors before you begin any job. Hiring the right contractor can go a long way in giving you peace of mind, when you are a Real Estate investor.

Chapter 8

A Master Blueprint For Getting "Peace of Mind Tenants

BLUEPRINT FOR TENANTS

A reminder for all matters and topics in this book consult an attorney or other qualified professionals.

Getting Rental Contracts made and signed

A rental agreement is a short-term contract, usually month to month. It can be written or verbal.

A lease is a written agreement that specifies the length and cost of the rent each month for that period.

You should have an attorney that specializes in lease agreements, make up your contracts.

If you decide to do it yourself here are web site s

that have templates for every state in the United States.

Nationwide Rental Lease Agreements

https://rentalleaseagreements.com/residential/

Rocket Lawyer Free Lease Agreements

https://goo.gl/vQGTEz

BLUEPRINT FOR TENANTS

How to Screen Prospective Tenants

Credit Score

Check the credit score of any prospective tenants. The credit score can show and ability to pay and a willingness to take responsiblity to pay obligations.

Steady Employment

Use paystubs and bank statements as proof of steady employment and the ability to pay.

Income Ratio

Income ratio should be about 3 times the amount of the rent.

Background Check

For your safety and the safety of any other tenants, do not skip on doing a background check.

BLUEPRINT FOR TENANTS

How to Screen Prospective Tenants

Prior Evictions

Check for prior evictions. Make sure another property manager is not trying to pass their problem off on you.

Valid Credentials

Make sure that all identification and credentials match up. Some times people attempt to rent property in other peoples names.

References

Check references thoroughly. Make sure that family and friends are not posing as prior landlords or work supervisors.

Reason for Moving

Ask the prospective tenant what was his reason for moving from his last residence. It may give you some insight into what kind of tenant you are going to have.

BLUEPRINT FOR TENANTS

Money – Money - Money

Collecting rent

There are several ways to collect rent. Below are a few of the more common and popular ones.

Online or ACH

automated clearing house payments

This is by far, the most convenient for you. One such company is Agile Payments.

https://www.agilepayments.com/

Drop Off Box

Just have a secured drop off box at a office on the property grounds.

By Mail

Make sure that the tenant is aware that payment by mail still has to be received by the due date.

BLUEPRINT FOR TENANTS

How to Handle Tenant Complaints

Make sure that tenants must put ALL COMPLAINTS in writing. Letter or email. Make no verbal agreements! Respond to complaints as quickly as possible. Make sure that any contract that responds to any proplem only makes repairs authorized by you.

Common Complaints and How to Handle Them

Neighbor Complaints

Start with a phone call and get the accused side of the story. If that does not work, do a field inspection to verify any complaint. If the complaint is valid, send the accused a letter citing what ever lease violation they have committed, and the consequences if such behavior continues.

Pests

Most common pest complaint is roaches, mice and bed bugs. First make sure that you begin with no pests. Call a contractor or maintenance person. Have the contractor or maintance person determine who or what is the cause of the pests.

BLUEPRINT FOR TENANTS

How to Handle Tenant Complaints

If it is the resident, let them know that it is a violation of their lease and they may have to pay for future pest removal.

Plumbling

The most common plumbing complaint is a toilet clog. Have a maintance person or a contractor repair the clog. Sometimes tenant flush things like diapers and other inappropriate things down the toilet. Make sure that your lease agreement forbids such behavior.

Temperature Control

Have your maintenance person check the temperature. Many states have regulations on temperature, so you might want to invest in temperature lock out devices that don't allow the tenant to set the temperature.

BLUEPRINT FOR TENANTS

How to Handle Tenant Complaints

Appliances

A refrigerator, stove or dish washer are the most common appliance complaints. Refrigerator repairs have priority, because food can spoil.

Hire a good appliance repair man. A repair can often save a fortune compared to a replacement.

Grounds

Getting a roof leak, a full dumpster, grass cut or snow removal is a common complaint. If you have these jobs contracted out, request a before and after photo of work done. Ice is particularly dangerous. You could get sued if someone injures themselves slipping on your property. Make sure you have reliable snow removal in place. Your maintenance team or a contractor should be able to handle most complaints about the grounds.

BLUEPRINT FOR TENANTS

How to Handle Tenant Complaints

Preventative Maintenance & Summary

Have maintenance outlined in your lease. This will assist you in preventive maintenance.

* Remember, everything must be in writing.

* The complaint must be in writing.

* You must respond in writing.

* When will the work be done.

* Who will be doing the work.

* Tenants will not be allowed to select a contractor.

* No repair work will be done without your authorization.

* No verbal agreements.

* Document multiple request for the same work to help reduce frivoulous calls and requests.

* State that the request gives you permission to enter the property.

BLUEPRINT FOR TENANTS

Dealing With Problem Tenants

"If you are brave enough to say goodbye, life will reward you with a new hello."

Paulo Coelho

Tenant Problems

No matter how good a job you do screening you still may come across a problem tenant. Sometimes a tenant might lose a job or have a death in the family. Something that changes their ability to meet their lease requirements. Here are some tenant problems you need to be prepared for.

Not Paying Rent

You are running a for profit business not a charity, and the rent must be paid in order for you to sustain your business. So when rent is missed what should you do? Follow the process. Each state has a legal process to follow. In some states, you serve a 3 day notice to evict. Followed by a court date. Every state has their own process. Learn your state's process and follow it to the letter.

BLUEPRINT FOR TENANTS

Dealing With Problem Tenants

"It's not you, it's me..."

Structure your lease so that if you have a problem tenant you can send a notice to vacate by a certain date. Some landlords have to serve a notice to cease the violation before they can send a notice to vacate. So begin by making sure your lease is structured properly in the first place.

Probable reasons to call it quits with a tenant.

* Abusing The Dwelling

* Disturbing the peace and quiet

* Breaking occupant rules

It is much easier to remove a tenant that has not paid, then a tenant that is breaking lease laws. So make sure your lease is very detailed as to what the rules are and what will happen if the rules are broken.

Chapter 9

End Vacancy Worries with Expert Real Estate Marketing

Marketing for Vacancy

The first part to marketing for vacancy is to reduce the chance of vacancy in the first place. Treat the tenants you have to your highest level of customer service.

Begin by having a scheduled visit at least once a year. During the visit talk to the tenant and ask them what you can do to make their stay in your property better. Make sure that when you schedule the visit you have also scheduled some form of improvement to the property. Let them see you caring for them with action, not just words. Change the air filter, paint a room, replace an appliance.

Give gifts. Offer your tenants referral fees. Let them know that it's something in it for them if they help keep your properties rented. Give your tenants a movie gift certificate for a family night out. Give the tenant a turkey or ham during the holidays, along with a thank you card, showing how much you appreciate their business. How much does a turkey cost? How much does one month of a vacant property cost?

If you are renting single family homes, offer a "rent to own" contract. Usually lasting two to three years. This gives the renter time to save money and establish credit.

Marketing for Vacancy

Offer rent incentives for the tenant to stay longer. For example, a twelve month lease is $800 a month, a eighteen month lease is $775 a month, a twenty four month lease is $750 a month.

Now that you have done all that you can to treat the tenants you have properly, you have to focus on filling vacant rental property.

Begin by viewing the federal fair housing act of 1968. Make sure that your ads or policies are not in violation of this law. You can view this document at this web site.

Https:www.hud.gov/

Then type "fair housing" in the search box.

Begin with the new basics in the age of the internet. Create a web site. Over %70 of people looking for a place to stay, begin online. Have a well written ad.

AIDA copy writing marketing formula. Get their **Attention** with a good headline. Increase their **Desire** and **Interest** with good benefits. Initiate Action with a call to **Action**.

Have all the detailed information abut your rental property on the web site. Have good clear photographs.

Marketing for Vacancy

Create a video of your property. If possible shoot a well lit clear video tour of your property. Have your address and location, your phone number and list all unit amenities. Show the rent, the deposit required and any additional charges. This will reduce phone calls and unnecessary questions.

Begin advertising your vacancy before it is vacant. Start advertising your rental property as soon as you are given notice of a lease ending.

Place a sign on the property, letting everybody know there is a place available for rent. Have a web site address on the sign for more information.

Use internet listing services. Here are a few of the top services.

HotPads

HotPads is a map-based rental property & real estate marketplace. They have been around for over a decade. They began in November 2005. The site allows users to search for housing using an interactive map.

Https://hotpads.com/

Marketing for Vacancy

Craigslist

Craigslist is an American nationwide classified advertisements web site with sections devoted to jobs, housing and a variety of things. They get up to 50 million views each month.

Https://craigslist.org

Cozy

The Cozy web site is an amazing utility for your rental property business. It allows you to set up rent collection, tenant screening, place property listings, rental applications, estimate rent, insurance, expense tracking and maintenance.

Http://goo.gl/gEu5Ey

Zillow Rental Manager

The Zillow rental manager is a great place for extending your education in the Rental Property Business. The resource section of the Zillow Rental Manager has information on becoming a landlord, managing your rental, landlord laws and regulations, webinars, and tools and forms.

Https://www.zillow.com/rental-manager/

Marketing for Vacancy

Use newspapers. Another way to increase your property exposure is to place ads in newspapers, but only if you are getting a good advertising rate. Papers can be expensive and news paper circulation is dropping, but if you are the only fish in a small pond, you get all the attention.

Use Google. Use Google to search for local rental property. See where your competitors are advertising for tenants. Duplicate some or all of the places they are advertising.

Use local library and college bulletin boards. Place a three by five card or a business card with your web site and contact information on it.

Use word of mouth. Carry business cards to give away to family and friends or associates at networking events.

In summary, do the best you can to keep the tenants you have. Set up a web site that has as much detailed information as possible, allowing you to qualify tenants without wasting your time. Use rental listing services and local advertising to maximize exposure to your property and end any vacancy as quickly as possible.

Chapter 10
Find low cost Rental Property Insurance

BUSINESS INSURANCE

Consult an attorney for any and all of your business matters.

In the early 1990's an elderly woman purchased a hot cup of coffee from a McDonald's drive-thru window in Albuquerque. She spilled the coffee, and suffered 3rd degree burns. She sued Mcdonald's and won. She won 2.7 million dollars in a punitive damages victory. The verdict was appealed and settlement is estimated at somewhere in the neighborhood of $500,000 dollars. All because she spilled the coffee into her lap, while trying to add sugar and cream.

Two men in Ohio, were carpet layers. They were severely burned when a three and a half gallon container of carpet adhesive ignited, when the hot water heater it was sitting next to, was turned on. They felt the warning lable on the back of the can was insufficient. So they filed a lawsuit against the adhesive manufacturers and were awarded nine million dollars.

A woman in Oklahoma, purchased a brand new Winnebago. While driving it home, she set the cruise control to 70 miles per hour. She then left the drivers seat to make some coffee or a sandwich in the back of the motor home.

BUSINESS INSURANCE

The vehicle crashed and the woman sued Winnebago for not advising her, that cruise control does not drive and steer the vehicle. She won 1.7 million dollars and the company had to rewrite their instruction manual.

Unfortunately all three outrageous lawsuits are real. If you are going to run a business, any business, you should consider protecting yourself with Professional Liability Insurance, also known as Errors and Omissions (E & 0) insurance.

This type of insurance can help to protect you from having to pay the full cost of defending yourself against a negligence lawsuit claim.

Error and Omissions can protect you against claims that are not usually covered in regular liability insurance. Those policies usually cover bodily harm, or damage to property. Error and Omissions can protect you agaist negligence, and other mental anguish like inaccurate advice, or misrepresentation. Criminal prosecution is not covered.

Errors and Ommision insurance is recommended for notaries public, real estate brokers or investors and professionals like: software engineers, lawyers, home inspectors web site delvelopers and landscape architects to name a few professions.

BUSINESS INSURANCE

The Most Common Errors and Omission Claims:

%25 Breach of Fiduciary Duty

%15 Breach of Contract

%14 Negligence

%13 Failure to Supervise

%11 Unsuitability

%10 Other

BUSINESS INSURANCE

Things you should know about or require before purchasing a Errors and Omission policy is...

* What is the limit of liability

* What is the Deductible

* Does it include FDD First Dollar Defense - which obligates the insurance company to fight a case without a deductible first.

* Do I have Tail-end coverage or Extended Reporting Coverage (insurance that lasts into retirement)

* Extended coverage for Employees

* Cyber Liability Coverage

* Department of Labor Fiduciary Coverage

* Insolvency Coverage

If you get Errors and Omission insurance, renew it the day it expires. You must be careful to avoid gaps in your coverage, or it could result in not getting your policy renewed.

BUSINESS INSURANCE

A few E & O Insurance Providers:

Insureon

Insureon states that their median Errors and Omissions Insurance policy cost about $750 a year or about $65 a month. The price of course will vary according to your business, the policy you choose and other risk factors.

https://www.insureon.com/home

EOforless

EOforless.com helps insurance, investment, and real estate professionals buy E & O insurance at an affordable cost in five minutes or less.

https://www.eoforless.com/

BUSINESS INSURANCE

CalSurance Associates

As a leading insurance broker, CalSurance Associates, a division of Brown & Brown Program Insurance Services, Inc. has over fifty years of experience delivering comprehensive insurance products, exceptional service, and proven results to over 150,000 insured. They provide professionals nationwide and across multiple industries, including some of the largest financial firms and insurance companies in the United States.

http://www.calsurance.com/csweb/index.aspx

Better Safe Than Sorry

Insurance is one of the hidden costs of doing business. These are just a few companies and a brief overview on the topic of business insurance. Make sure to talk to an attorney or quailified insurance agent before making any decision on insurance. Protect you and your business. Many states do not require E & O insurances. But when you see the cost of some of the settlements, it's better to be safe than sorry.

$10,000

Massive Money Internet Marketing &

Copy Writing & SEO Course &

$1,000 Value Bonus

Internet Marketing Videos

LIBRARY I (Video Training Programs)

1. Product Creation
2. Copy Writing & Payment
3. Auto Responder & Product Download Page
4. How to start a Freelancing business
5. Video Marketing
6. List Building
7. Affiliate Marketing
8. How to Get Massive Web Site Traffic

LIBRARY II (Video Training Programs)

1. Goldmine Government Grants
2. How to Write a Business Plan
3. Secrets to making money on eBay
4. Credit Repair
5. Goal Setting
6. Asset Protection How to Incorporate

$10,000 MegaSized Internet Marketing &

Copy Writing & SEO Course &

$1,000 Value Bonus

Library III
1. **SEO SIMPLIFIED PART 1**
2. **SEO SIMPLIFIED PART 2**
3. **SEO Private Network Blogs**
4. **SEO Social Signals**
5. **SEO Profits**

Bonus 1000 Package!
1. **Insider Secrets to Government Contracts (PDF)**
2. **1000 Books/Guides (text files)**
3. **Vacation Discounts (text file w/links to discounts)**
4. **Media Players (3 Software Programs)**
100% MONEY BACK GUARANTEE!!!
ALL ON A 8 GIGABYTE FLASH DRIVE

This Massive Library with a $10,000 value all for only a

1 time payment of $67!!!

Get Instant Access by Using the Link Below:

https://urlzs.com/p7v3T

Leave a review and join Our VIP Mailing List Then Get All our Audio Books Free! We will be releasing over 100 money making audio books within the next 12 months! Just leave a review and join our mailing list and get them all for free!

Just Hit/Type in the Link Below

https://urlzs.com/HfbGF